THE MARITIME PROVINCES

RUPERT O. MATTHEWS

THE IMAGE BANK®

The Image Bank® is a registered trademark of
The Image Bank, Inc.

Copyright © The Image Bank 1989. All rights reserved.
No part of this publication may be reproduced,
stored in a retrieval system, transmitted,
or used in any form or by any means,
electronic, mechanical, photocopying, recording
or otherwise without the prior permission
of the copyright holder.

ISBN 0-941267-11-3

Manufactured in Spain

Producer : Ted Smart
Author : Rupert O. Matthews
Book Design : Sara Cooper
Photo Research : Ed Douglas
Production Assistant : Seni Glaister

Newfoundland

If there is a single area in all the Americas which can be said to be truly distinctive it is the eastern seaboard of Canada, the famous Maritime Provinces. They are so individual that they do not even share a common culture among themselves. Each of the four provinces, indeed each region within the provinces, has a flavour and a culture all its own. There is nowhere quite like the Maritimes.

The strangely individual atmosphere of the area is as much due to the land and the sea as to its people, and dates back to the earliest days of European settlement. It was in 1497 that John Cabot, an Italian sailor working for England's King Henry VII, first sighted the towering cliffs and deep inlets of a rocky island he named the New Found Land. Today many residents pay tribute to the nature of the island by ignoring the name given to it by Cabot and referring to it simply as The Rock.

In fact Cabot was not particularly interested in the bleak, rugged and magnificent land he had discovered. He was much more excited by the seas around it. He found that all he needed to do was throw a wicker basket overboard and haul it in to catch a hefty load of cod. The possibilities of the find were great, but first Cabot had to find a harbour. On St John's Day, Cabot discovered a narrow crack in a line of cliffs. Nosing his ship through the gap Cabot found a magnificent harbour. He named it St John's and claimed it for England. Scarcely bothering to land, Cabot turned for home, anxious to tell his news.

The king and his courtiers were disappointed that no gold had been found, but the merchants of Bristol listened eagerly to the stories about fish. They knew a profit-making possibility when they heard it and immediately got a fleet together. They found the seas around Newfoundland to be every bit as rich as Cabot had said.

Southeast of the island the sea is unusually shallow for several hundred miles away from the land. These shallows, known as the Banks, mark the meeting of two great oceanic currents. Running down from the west coast of Greenland the chilly Labrador current brings nutrient-rich water down from the Arctic. Flowing northward from Florida the warm Gulf Stream runs head on into the Labrador Current. The colder waters are forced downwards, where they strike the shallow floor of the Banks. Unable to escape, the two great currents mix and mingle. The rich cold waters are warmed by the Gulf Stream. Plankton thrive in the warm, productive mix and grow in amazing quantity. Vast schools of fish are attracted by the plankton and swarm in the waters.

No fish is more characteristic of the Grand Banks than the cod. This large fish can measure over four feet in length and weigh over 100 pounds. With its soft white underbelly and dark brown speckled back, the cod has become "the fish" in Newfoundland. If the visitor sees fish on a menu it means cod. Other fish are referred to by name.

The Newfies, as natives of the rugged island are known, have developed a multitude of ways of cooking the cod. It may be simply carved into thick steaks and grilled, or it can be steamed or fried and bathed in a variety of sauces. Cod tongues, often poached in milk, have become a noted local delicacy. They are said to lose their subtle flavour within twenty four hours of the fish leaving the sea, so they are a dish unlikely to become popular far beyond the shores of the island.

The early fishermen did not settle on Newfoundland. They came in the spring, landed to establish seasonal bases and returned home. The shore bases served as small boatyards, store depots and processing plants where the fish were split open and laid out to dry in the sun. According to tradition the first captain to reach a particular anchorage at the start of each season became the Fishing Admiral. He enforced justice and organised the fishing, taking a percentage for his trouble. By the late 16th century 30,000 fishermen came to the Banks each year.

When, in 1583, England laid formal claim to Newfoundland, the system of Fishing Admirals was formalised and given the backing of law. At first settlement was discouraged, the Bristol merchants wanted no rivals at all. But colonists arrived nonetheless. Most of them came from Ireland and England's western counties. The soft burr of their accents can still be found in the idiosyncratic speech of the Newfies.

Not only the accents of the first settlers, but also their words and sayings have been preserved. Nowhere else does such a pure form of 17th century English remain. Sayings familiar to Shakespeare have been liberally spiced with local terms redolent of the fishing business. A Newfie being told to keep a long draw on his big jib would understand that he was being wished luck.

These people settled in the narrow inlets and craggy harbours which abound around the coast of Newfoundland. Many of which were only accessible by boat and remain cut off from any roads to this day. Isolated on their Rock for generation upon generation the Newfies built up a culture dependent upon the local resources and their own inventiveness.

Through the centuries the sea remained the dominant influence. It provided the people with their livelihoods; its rhythms regulated their lives. The traditional cycle of the fishing year got under way in May when the sea ice breaks up. For a few short weeks the salmon run filled the seas with thousands of fish. The men put out from the villages in big open boats powered by six rowers each to catch the valuable fish. The salmon could be smoked and cured before being sold to merchants. Most of the cash was made in these few short weeks.

In early summer the 'caplin run' began, and the real fishing got under way. Caplin are small fish not highly valued as food, but they are the prey of the cod. When the caplin come inshore to breed, the huge schools of cod follow. Large nets were laid out in squares to catch the cod as they moved inshore. The haul was enormous and the villagers worked every daylight hour to get the fish landed, cleaned and dried. By July the caplin run was over, but most fishermen had caught the majority of their year's catch.

Later in the season, the cod moved out on to the Grand Banks, hundreds of miles from shore. The schooners would go out, carrying small dories. The dories did the actual fishing, while the schooners acted as salting plants. The pair of men in each dory paid out long lines festooned with jiggers, hooks attached to bright metal tabs which swing and dance in the current and are irresistible to cod.

Often the schooners, and the menfolk of a village, would be at sea for the entire summer, not returning until the winter ice began to close in. In the days before radio, this meant a long, anxious wait for the families at home. As winter came in, the age old tasks of repairing nets and boats took over.

The isolated fishing villages were backed by only a small area of cultivatable land. Here the women tended tiny vegetable patches while the men were out on the Banks. It was a tough and a hard life, but a colourful culture was developed. The folksongs of Ireland and the West Country were kept alive, and many new ones developed. Perhaps inevitably these dealt with the sea and the ships and the men who serve them. Often the songs had accompanying dances, ranging from graceful square dances to wild and uninhibited jigs and reels.

When, in 1949, Newfoundland joined itself to Canada, by a majority of just 4% of the vote, things began to change. Government and corporation money came in to finance large scale fishing enterprises. Trawlers replaced the schooners and dories on the Banks while processing plants producing frozen fish fingers took the place of drying racks. The catching of cod has become big business. Many villagers have forsaken the sea for more highly paid jobs offered by government and large companies from central Canada.

But there are still many lone fishermen putting to sea in small boats, now motorised rather than oar-powered. They catch cod during the caplin run in modern gill-nets, but most of their efforts are concentrated on other catches. Salmon are as valuable as ever, but today squid finds a ready sale on the international markets. The lobsters which abound on the rocky coasts of Newfoundland are being caught in larger numbers than ever before, and shipped west to Canada.

Newfoundland has the highest proportion of native-born inhabitants of any province, perhaps because the beautiful, rugged land exerts a special hold. Some still live in the 'outposts', the villages with such odd names as Heart's Desire, Witless Bay and Little Heart's Ease, but many others have moved to the city of St John's and the new industrial bases which have sprung up in recent years.

St John's was the first permanent settlement on the Rock, and until recent years was the only town of any size. At the centre of the city, is its whole reason for being; the harbour. The open stretch of water is over a mile in length and nearly half as wide, yet it opens in to the ocean through a gap barely 700 feet across. The opening is flanked by spectacular cliffs over 500 feet high which rise to form the heights which dominate the town.

The northern cliff rises to a hill known as Signal Hill, one of the most historic spots in Newfoundland. During the 18th century Seven Years War, the British fortified the hill to protect the harbour, and saw ferocious fighting with the French. During the War of 1812 the defences were updated and extended, creating the maze of gun emplacements, batteries and trenches which can still be seen today. Less than fifty years ago Signal Hill was recommissioned by the military to guard St John's from sneak attacks by Nazi U-boats.

On a more peaceful tone, Signal Hill was the site where the very first transatlantic radio signal was received. In 1901 Guglielmo Marconi set up a transmitter in Cornwall, then travelled to St John's where he managed to pick up the letter 'S' transmitted in Morse code.

Clustered along the western side of the harbour is the Old City. The street plan of old St John's is one of the most haphazard on the continent. Over the long centuries of the fishing trade little thought was given to the roads and paths of the growing community, they were simply allowed to meander wherever was most convenient at the time. The result is a collection of narrow, twisting cobbled lanes and streets which may be picturesque but is totally unsuited to the demands of modern traffic.

Most of the old city was built of wood and has been destroyed by a series of fires over the years. However several important buildings remain, mostly those built in stone. The Classical-style Colonial building was, until recently, the seat of the Provincial Assembly and now houses state papers. Government House is more of a home, being built along Georgian lines and set within broad gardens.

Perhaps the most noticeable landmark in the city is the Catholic Basilica of St John. Its twin 140 foot towers rise above the houses, dominating the skyline with a stolid security which echoes the atmosphere of the whole city. Within the church is one of the most touching sights in the Maritimes. It is a small statue, identical to that standing at Fatima in Portugal where an important vision of the Virgin Mary was received by some peasant children. The statue was presented to the Basilica by a group of Portuguese sailors whose fishing ship was wrecked on the Grand Bank and who only survived by what they considered to be a miracle. The statue was presented in thanks.

St John's is built on one of the deep inlets which characterise Newfoundland. Indeed the whole island may be thought of as a series of inlets and peninsulas linked by stretches of land. The city stands at the tip of Avalon Peninsula, one of the largest, which stretches over sixty miles from its narrow neck. It is only twenty years since the road linking the Avalon Peninsula with the far side of the Province at Corner Brook was actually sealed. Before that date it had been a gravel track which bad weather made impassable.

The road winds around the northern coast of Newfoundland, cutting across the neck of the picturesque Bonavista Peninsula before plunging into the Terra Nova National Park. Spread over 150 square miles, Terra Nova includes some of the island's most spectacular terrain. There are dozens of long, narrow bays and inlets carved by ice many thousands of years ago, and during the winter icebergs float close offshore as the Labrador Current brings them down from Greenland. It was one of these bergs which, in 1912, sank the Titanic with the loss of 1,500 lives.

Just west of Terra Nova is the town of Gander. Now a quiet backwater, Gander was once a major stopover on the Atlantic air routes. Before the introduction of large jet planes, aircraft could not cross the ocean in one leap. They had to stop over at Newfoundland to refuel. Gander was the airfield chosen for its long runway and large fuel stores. The airport can still be seen, but the business has moved on.

More ancient in its transatlantic connections is l'Anse aux Meadows at the northernmost point of the island. Here, on a grassy slope, a few foundations and a wrecked smithy are all that remain of the first European settlement in Canada. It was here that Vikings from Greenland landed to fell timber for transport home. Their adventures are celebrated in Icelandic sagas. Though the more colourful storylines of the sagas, with their blood fueds and heroic deeds, cannot be verified, l'Anse aux Meadows at least proves that they came here. The settlement has been rebuilt a short distance away, recreating the sod houses and smoky fires of the Vikings.

The Vikings would have felt at home on Newfoundland for much of the scenery is reminiscent of their native Norway. Nowhere is this more true than at Gros Morne, where the fjords of Scandinavia are reproduced. The immensely ancient Long Range mountains have been ground down over the eons to produce a flat-topped plateau over 2,500 feet in height. During the Ice Ages great glaciers formed inland and ground down towards the coast. As they moved, they gouged out the deep, U-shaped valleys so characteristic of Gros Morne.

The most spectacular of the true fjords is Bonne Bay, which extends many miles inland along a narrow path cut through the massif by the glaciers. To the north lies Western Brook Pond, a lake formed in the floor of a huge glaciated valley with cliffs towering over 2,000 feet above the waterlevel. Only the fact that this is a fresh water lake, separated from the ocean by a short stream, stops this being the greatest fjord in Canada.

Nova Scotia

South of Gros Morne the main highway runs along the spectacular coast, passing Corner Brook and Stephenville to reach Port aux Basques. Here the road stops. It can go no further. Travellers must take to the ferry which leaves regularly to sail to North Sydney on Cape Breton Island.

Though the name of the port might suggest an Australian influence, the names of nearby settlements reveal the true cultural heritage of the area. Lone Shieling, Clyde and Mackenzie Mountain speak of the Scottish background to the region. Indeed the province is known as Nova Scotia, Latin for New Scotland.

Between 1770 and 1830 the crofters, or small farmers, of the Scottish Highlands were evicted to make way for more economic large scale farming. Many clan chiefs and landlords paid for the dispossessed Scots to sail to the New World to make a new home for themselves. The first boatload of 200 Highlanders arrived at Pictou in 1773. More than 50,000 men, women and children followed in a few years.

On Cape Breton Island the Scots found a land very much like that they had left behind. The soaring mountains were covered with thin grass and scrubby heather, ideal for sheep grazing, while the patches of sheltered lowland produced abundant crops of barley and oats.

The Scots settled in quickly, establishing their culture here as firmly as in the lands they had left. To this day the people of Cape Breton are identifiably Scottish. There is a flourishing weaving business which produces tartans and tweeds after traditional patterns. Many towns and villages stage Highland Games where locals don the kilts and sporrans of their ancestors. Among the many contests are those for Highland dancing and pipe playing. The pipes in question are, of course, the strident bagpipes which evolved in the windswept mountains of northern Scotland.

The most distinctive sport, however, is tossing the caber. Contrary to most throwing competitions the aim is not to hurl the caber as far as possible. The art, and skill, lies in getting the caber to land on its end and turn over in a straight line with the throw. Only the most proficient can achieve a perfectly straight toss.

Other traditions have been kept alive in Cape Breton, of which one of the most pervasive is the music. Not only do the pipes echo across the mountains, but the folksongs of Scotland are still to be heard at dances and in halls. Indeed, some of the finest singers of Scottish folksongs have come from Cape Breton. The island has also produced a fresh crop of songs, based on the old patterns, which celebrate the new homeland and its beauties. Many of these songs are in Gaelic, a language still spoken in some of the more out of the way villages and officially encouraged at the Gaelic College in St Anns. At the suitably named Iona, the Nova Scotia Highland Village Museum recreates the houses and byres built by the earliest Scottish settlers together with their arts and crafts.

The rugged beauty of Cape Breton has made the island a popular tourist resort, and no attraction is more popular than the Cabot Trail. This 180 mile round trip runs around the Cape North Peninsula, taking in some of the most magnificent views in the province. The route is named after John Cabot, who discovered the island in 1497, but it only came into being in recent years.

The terrain of the peninsula is rocky and mountainous in the extreme. Most of the coastal settlements through which it runs were accessible only by sea until less than a hundred years ago. By the beginning of this century a rough track wound around the cliff tops and through the high passes, but few used it. A few daredevils attempted the route in motorcars during the 20s, but it was not a journey for the fainthearted. In places the unsurfaced track ran along routes where sheer drops plummeted over 1,000 feet to the sea on one side and mountains rose high on the other.

Even today the Cabot Trail is something of an adventure. The old cartracks and footpaths have been widened and surfaced to take motor traffic, but the heart-stopping drops and gear-grinding hills remain. Most travellers prefer to journey clockwise so as to be on the inside when traversing the more hair-raising cliff roads of the coast. One of the most amazing stretches is the two mile run leading down from Cape Smokey, during which the road drops 1,200 feet in a series of hairpin bends and short straights.

One of the interesting places passed by the Cabot Trail is Baddeck, on the shores of a lake which closely resembles a Scottish loch. It was here that the Scottish inventor, Alexander Graham Bell made his home. After inventing the telephone in 1876, Bell had enough money to give up his teaching post and wsa able to devote himself to his researches full time. He bought a property at Baddeck and named it Beinn Bhreagh, Gaelic for Beautiful Mountain. He worked on aids for the deaf and was a moving spirit behind the first flight by aircraft to be made in Canada and the invention of the hydrofoil craft. He died here in August 1922 and his house is preserved as a museum to his life and works.

But the Scots were not the first settlers on Cape Breton. If today they are the dominant cultural force, it is only because they arrived last and in greatest numbers. On the island's southeast coast are very definite signs of earlier settlers; the great French fortress of Louisbourg.

In the early 18th century the French settlers owned most of inland Canada, but were dependent on the shipping using the St Lawrence River for contact with the homeland. King Louis XV decided to construct Louisbourg to safeguard the route. It was to be a fortified naval base from which ships could put out to protect French merchantmen sailing between Canada and France.

The plan was for a large, angular fortress containing a town and surrounded by farmlands extensive enough to feed the town and to resupply the ships which called. The fortress quickly took shape and became a bastion of French power in eastern Canada. In 1758 the British determined to capture Louisbourg. Led by General Wolfe, who was later to capture Quebec, the British army took Louisbourg, slighted its defences and left it in ruins.

Today the fortress has been restored to its days of glory in the 1740s, when it was a cornerstone of French Canada. Many of the defences have been rebuilt, together with the great fortified gateways. The largest single building is the King's Bastion, more a barracks than a bastion, where the richly furnished Governor's Residence has been fully restored along with the more humble soldiers' quarters. The whole complex, embracing dozens of rebuilt structures, is staffed by people in period costume. They live out the lives of the original inhabitants, carrying on crafts and skills of the day.

It was largely because of the threat posed by Louisbourg that the British began their own fortress town some miles to the west at Halifax. Belonging to the victorious power, Halifax did not suffer the destruction and abandonment which afflicted Louisbourg. It has remained a thriving city from its founding in 1749 to the present day.

The city is dominated, both physically and historically, by the Citadel. It was on this steep crag that Lord Cornwallis built his fortress in the summer of 1749 to protect the harbour. Over the years the strongpoint has been demolished and rebuilt four times to keep up with the changing military technology. Most recently the Citadel was reworked last century as a massive artillery battery able to sink any ship which entered the harbour and capable of withstanding a long siege. It is almost disappointing to find that these impressive defences were never put to the test.

The military have long since abandoned the Citadel, finding more effective ways than muzzle-loading cannon to sink ships, but the structure continues to be used. It is now a National Historic Park and its sturdy stone defences have been restored to period excellence. The ramparts and emplacements are as strong as when first built, and the dry moat which surrounds the Citadel can be seen to be a death trap. Any attacking infantry who reached the ditch would be enfiladed by musket fire and cannon positioned to sweep the area.

Together with the defences, many interior rooms have been restored, including the magazine, the barracks and the officers' quarters. Guides take visitors on tours through the Citadel which, in the darker recesses of the fortress, rely on the candles and oil lanterns of the period for illumination. During summer afternoons a group of volunteers recreates the drills and musket practice of the period when the fortress was finally completed.

On the slopes below the Citadel is the Town Clock, which has come to be the symbol of Halifax. Though the exact origins of the truncated building are rather obscure, it is said that the clock was erected on the orders of Prince Edward, Duke of Kent, who commanded Halifax for six years early last century. Kent was famous as a punctual man who never forgave lateness in those who served him. Perhaps he believed that with the Town Clock to guide them, no resident of Halifax need ever be late again. The structure was restored in 1962 and continues to keep excellent time.

On the waterfront below the Town Clock is a small area of Halifax which has become famous as the Historic Properties. Just twenty years ago it was planned to flatten the area to build a much needed highway along the waterfront. But when it was pointed out that the buildings scheduled for demolition were among the oldest in the nation the plans were abandoned and the area was earmarked for an exciting project.

The buildings were restored and renovated as shops, restaurants and museums. Among other buildings there is the Old Red Store, built in 1812. It was constructed specifically to cater for the privateers who put out from Halifax. Privateers were warships owned by private citizens which served during wartime for no pay. They were, however, allowed to keep any enemy property they could capture. The Nova Scotian privateers made a speciality of snapping up American and French merchant ships, laden with rich cargoes. The loot was brought back to Halifax, stored in the Privateers Warehouse, now a jazz club, and sold in the Old Red Store. The coming of peace in 1815 meant the end of a lucrative trade for Halifax.

The many charming buildings of the Historic Properties region are fortunate in that they survived two catastrophes to strike Halifax. The first was a fire which devastated most of the city in 1859. The second was even worse, being the largest explosion known to the pre-nuclear world. During World War I, Halifax served as a vital port for the movement of war materials from Canada and the United States to Britain and France.

In December 1917 the French merchantman *Mont Blanc* loaded up with a large cargo of TNT, guncotton and benzol. While moving through the Narrows the *Mont Blanc* collided with a Belgian ship, the *Imo*. The French ship was badly damaged and caught fire. The crew fled, but before they could raise the alarm the huge cargo of explosives erupted in a blast which was heard over 100 miles away. Nearly half the houses in the town were destroyed, killing 2,000 people and wounding 10,000 more. The *Mont Blanc* virtually ceased to exist. Its anchor was eventually found over 2 miles away, but of the ship itself nothing could be found.

At the heart of Halifax is the spreading Fishermen's Market where shoppers can find every kind of fish which is caught off these coasts. In addition to the almost inevitable cod, there are flounders, haddock and the highly prized lobster. Nova Scotia is intimately connected with the lobster. Indeed some claim that the province is shaped like a lobster, the southern mass forming the body and the twin peninsulas of Cape Breton the claws.

The rocky coasts which surround Nova Scotia are ideal for the lobster. It is among the submerged rocks that the lobsters find the small animals and debris on which they feed. When threatened the lobster may retreat into a rocky hole where its soft underbelly cannot be reached. Clearly lobsters would be difficult creatures to catch.

Fortunately for the lobstermen, the lobster is willing to explore small spaces in its search for food. It is for this reason that the lobster pots are so successful. Wire or wicker cages with a narrow opening which can only be passed in one direction are baited and cast into the sea. The lobster, sensing the bait, enters the pot and then finds that it cannot leave. When the fisherman returns some hours later he finds a lobster in his pot.

The cooks of Nova Scotia have a particular affinity with the lobster, being able to serve it up in a wide variety of mouthwatering dishes. But perhaps the best way to eat lobster is still simply to boil it and serve it with a generous slice of lemon.

The lobster pots are to be found stacked high on wooden wharves at the many villages which run around the coasts of Nova Scotia. In some places the pots take on the appearance of towering buildings they are so numerous. Famed as perhaps the most picturesque of all the fishing villages is Peggy's Cove.

Lying on a wide bay on the southern coast, Peggy's Cove is a cluster of clapboard houses and fishing huts clustered around a maze of quiet inlets and rocky shores. Though there is a seemingly unending stream of visitors to this village through the summer months, the peaceful isolation of the area remains largely unspoilt. This may be due to the area's protected status enforced by law. The name of the village is said to come from a survivor of a shipwreck who came ashore here, married a local man and never went home again.

Off the coast a few miles from Peggy's Cove is the mysterious Oak Island. In 1795 a local boy named Daniel McGinnis landed on the uninhabited island on a fishing trip. What he found began a quest which has continued to the present day. In the centre of the island McGinnis discovered signs of digging. He returned the next day with some friends and began excavating. They soon found a layer of stones, and at a depth of ten feet a layer of logs. Ten feet further down they reached a second layer of logs, and a third at thirty feet. Then the pit flooded and they abandoned the attempt.

Locals recalled that over the previous century or so Nova Scotia had been the haunt of privateers and pirates. The idea spread that McGinnis had stumbled across a shaft leading to a fortune in buried treasure. Eager tunnellers congregated on the island and began digging. Over the following century many attempts were made to delve into the pit. In all eleven wooden platforms were found at ten foot intervals. At a depth of 140 feet an abandoned lantern and pick were found, below them was a layer of oak. It was discovered that the water in the pit entered by a complicated system of tunnels which connected to the open sea.

The most recent attempt to solve the riddle came in 1970 when a remote controlled TV camera was lowered to a depth of 220 feet. It seemed to show three battered wooden chests in a rock cavity, but the evidence was controversial. In 1989 a new excavation was launched with the aim of solving the mystery of the money pit.

Washing the northern shores of Nova Scotia are the waters of the Bay of Fundy, which nearly separate the province from the mainland at Amherst. The Bay is fished by many boats which haul in splendid catches of lobster and other shellfish, but the area is most famous for its tides. Because of the configuration of the seabed and the sudden narrowing of the Bay the tidal flow is particularly strong. On average the tides rise and fall over 40 feet twice a day. During extreme spring tides, the waters may top 54 feet between high and low tide. It is not at all unusual for fishermen to unload their craft using duckboards laid over mud, then wait a few hours and sail out across the same mud, now covered by seawater.

New Brunswick

Beyond the Bay of Fundy lies New Brunswick, the birthplace of one of the most enduring folkheroes of North America. This was Paul Bunyan, a logger said to be able to fell a tree with the backswing of his axe as well as with the forward swing. He is credited with being a giant so tall that most men only reached his knees and so fast at felling that it took two dozen men with mules to haul away the timber he felled.

In truth Paul Bunyan was a hero of the lumberjacks. He had all the qualities they admired, only more so. In his developed form Paul Bunyan was a mythical giant, but that is not to say that many years ago there was not a real Paul Bunyan felling in the interior of New Brunswick, nor that he wasn't far better at the job than his fellows.

Early in the development of the stories about Paul Bunyan the tales were transported west to Michigan and the Rockies, and he is often thought of as an American creation. But the original tales come from New Brunswick. In one version of his birth it is said that it was the rocking of his cradle on a beach which set up the huge tides in the Bay of Fundy. The story continues that when he grew out of the cradle the Royal Navy took the wood and built seven warships with it. Such stories seem to date the early legends to the mid-18th century, or perhaps a few years earlier.

If Paul Bunyan were to return to New Brunswick today, he would find a land with which he would be familiar. Over 80% of the province is covered by standing timber. Some of the forests are located on inaccessible mountains and in remote valleys where lumbering is not a viable proposition. But along the Miramichi Valley lumbering is big business. Dense coniferous forests blanket the slopes above the river and the side valleys. Logging crews move through the dark woodlands, felling trees and shipping the timber out.

Most of the timber goes to the pulp and paper industries. Logs from the Miramichi are floated downstream to Newcastle where large sawmills convert the tree trunks to sawn timber and pulp. Timber felled on the Saint John River is floated down to Fredericton or processed at Edmunston. Smaller mills can be found scattered along the valley which process the timber in the forest prior to it being taken out by road.

In the last century the majority of the timber went to building ships in Saint John and other ports of the New Brunswick coast. These were the famous Bluenose ships which put out to sail the oceans of the world in search of trade. In fact the term 'Bluenose' originally referred to the men who sailed the ships through the cold waters off Canada's east coast and was only later transferred to the ships.

Drawing on the vast stands of timber in the interior, New Brunswick became one of the great international shipbuilding areas during the 19th century. At the time of Confederation, New Brunswick was one of the most populous and prosperous regions of Canada. The situation soon changed. The increasing use of steam engines and the introduction of cheap steel plates for ship hulls meant the end of New Brunswick's shipbuilding industry. By 1914 the last major yard had closed.

However, local shipyards have continued to produce inshore fishing boats, keeping alive the traditions of wooden craft construction. Those boats bring ashore a rich harvest from the seas. Lobster is as common here as in Nova Scotia, but the New Brunswickers have taken to farming the valuable crustacean in large caged pounds in bays and inlets. Other catches include clams, mussels, scallops, crabs and sardines together with the bluefin tuna.

The cooks of New Brunswick are able to convert the fresh catches into mouthwatering dishes. Most agree that the catches are best eaten on the wharves as soon as they are landed. Summer evenings in the fishing ports are heavy with the smell of chargrilling shad and cod or steaming pots of shellfish. At home, the larger fish are usually deepfried, but smaller dishes may be poached or steamed with a variety of accompaniments.

Among the more local sidedishes is dulse. Rather unappetising to the eye of a visitor, dulse is a species of purple seaweed which is collected on the rocky coasts and then laid out to dry on the seashore. It has a deliciously tangy flavour reminiscent of seabreezes wafting ashore on a spring evening.

Equally distinctive to New Brunswick kitchens is the fiddlehead fern. This plant grows in profusion around lakeshores and riverbanks during the spring and early summer. To be at its best the fiddlehead must be picked when its tender young fronds are half unwound, creating a shape similar to the head of a classical violin, or fiddle. Lightly boiled and then served with lemon juice and butter, the ferns perfectly complement the local seafood.

But the most idiosyncratic cookery of New Brunswick is that of the Acadians, most of whom live along the northern coast. Among the better known dishes are fricot, a braised chicken dish, and poutine rape, a dish of potatoes and pork. The delicacy of the Acadian cookery reveals the French heritage which it perpetuates, for the Acadians are the original European settlers of the province.

The early French explorers referred to the Maritime region as *Acadie* after a semi-mythical region of Ancient Greece where simple shepherds were said to live in perfect harmony with nature. Perhaps attracted by the romantic name, French settlers began arriving in the 1630s. They established farms and villages throughout the lands which are now Nova Scotia and New Brunswick and became a prosperous colonial population.

In 1713 Britain gained the region from the French. The Acadians were allowed to remain, so long as they took an oath of loyalty to the British Crown. But in the 1740s warfare flared up between France and Britain. When the French gained a surprise victory in 1747 at Grand Pre it was widely thought that they owed their success to local Acadian help. The Acadians were immediately deported to New England and Louisiana, or fled to Quebec. In Louisiana the name Acadian became corrupted to Cajun, the name for French settlers.

After the peace of 1763 many thousands of Acadians returned to eastern Canada, and most settled in New Brunswick. Today the Acadians make up some 40% of the provincial population and their cultural influence is strong. In the northeast of the province the population is so overwhelmingly French-speaking that the area is referred to as the Acadian Coast.

So proud of their Acadian forbears are the Maritimers that they have recreated two full scale Acadian villages. The first stands at Port Royal in Nova Scotia, where the first permanent French colony was established in 1605 by the explorer Samuel de Champlain. The new arrivals were determined to provide themselves with the comforts of home. They built snug houses, well fortified against attack, and established a social club and a theatre. Unfortunately for the Acadians, the British did not approve of the new settlement and destroyed it in 1613.

The fact that the site was not inhabited thereafter has meant that the archaeological evidence has not been disturbed by later buildings. Scientists have been able to study the lifestyle of the first Acadians, and to recreate it at Port Royal Habitation. Work began in 1939, relying heavily on the memoirs of Champlain and settlers.

The houses were built in a style then common in rural France. Massive horizontally-laid logs were built up within a framework of uprights and then clad with weatherboarding. This gave a solid, and pleasing structure. The roofs were steeply pitched and clad with shingles. Only the stone chimneys were not built of wood. The French were well aware that they might face attack from the Indians or the British at any time. The buildings were linked together and faced onto a central square. The exterior face of the Habitation being formed of tall, blank, easily defended walls.

New Brunswick's Acadian Historical Village, or more properly the Village Acadien Historique, near Grande-Anse is very much larger and more developed. It is not based upon any one settlement, but seeks to recreate many different aspects of Acadian culture from the period 1780-1880 in the one place. Staff, dressed in period costume, act as guides and continue to practice the traditional crafts of the Acadians. There are cod-salters, bakers and wheelwrights, among others.

The modern Acadian culture has moved forward into the technological age, as has the rest of New Brunswick. It can be best seen on the peninsula which has Caraquet resting on its tip. Caraquet, itself, is a small city almost devoted to fishing. The harbour is crowded with small wooden craft, built by local craftsmen using age old techniques, in which fishermen catch lobster and inshore fish. Fewer in number are the larger craft which put out into the Atlantic in search of cod and the bluefin tuna. There is even a Fisheries School which teaches youngsters the skills of modern fishing.

Caraquet is also the heartland of Acadian culture. During August the town celebrates its French ancestry in the Acadian Festival. The centre of the festival is the traditional Blessing of the Fleet, when a priest blesses the boats which take the men of Caraquet to sea in search of their catch. Other events include processions, folksong competitions and dances.

The coast around Caraquet is made up of spreading saltmarshes. The Acadians developed a unique and magnificently simple method of draining the saltmarshes and making them productive. The high tides of the region regularly inundate the low-lying land with seawater, adding salt to the soil and restricting plant growth to those tough grasses which can tolerate such conditions. However, fresh water streams flow into the marshes and these have created the conditions used by the ingenious Acadians.

Long dykes were built around the marshes and gates hinged horizontally so as to open outwards were placed in a few gaps in the dykes. When the tides rose the pressure of the water closed the gates, stopping the seawater from entering the marsh. When the tide fell the gates flapped open, allowing the freshwater streams to pour into the sea. Over many years the salt was washed from the soil and lush grasses grew where once there had been salt marsh. Cattle and sheep were driven on to the rich meadows to add to the economy of the region.

Beyond the marshes, the coast rises into a series of rocky headlands and sheltered bays. It is spectacularly beautiful and is among the most charming stretches of Canadian shores. It is off this section of coast that locals sometimes sight an old time sailing ship silently cruising by. It is widely accepted that this is a phantom, the ghostly recreation of the last voyage of a French man of war lost off the coast more than two centuries ago. As with other tales of phantom ships, however, the stories remain more interesting than substantial.

Buildings and festivals around Caraquet are often bedecked with the unofficial Acadian flag, a French tricolour bearing a yellow star in the upper left corner. The use of the flag is a constant reminder to visitors that though the Acadians count themselves Canadian they are acutely aware of their different cultural heritage.

Rather more jocular in origin is the eagle flag which waves over the lumber town of Edmunston in northwestern New Brunswick and the surrounding Madawaska County. The rich timber lands of the Upper Saint John River Valley were long a bone of contention between Quebec and New Brunswick. As soon as the United States became independent, Maine began to cast acquisitive eyes on the Saint John. The two Canadian provinces came to an amicable agreement whereby New Brunswick would own the valley but French Canadians from Quebec would be welcome to work the logging camps. It is said that the settlement was finally agreed over a game of dice between the two governors.

The Americans proved to be more difficult to keep out and sporadic border clashes were not uncommon. Canadian lumberjacks only had to catch Americans cutting timber on New Brunswick soil for fighting to break out. The fact that the American jacks protested that the land on which they stood should belong to Maine did little to appease the indignant Canadians. In 1842 the governments came to an agreement which gave Maine the valley above Fort Kent and the Canadians the lower valley.

The timbermen continued to poach timber from beyond the official border and the question 'Which nation are you from?' became a common, and suspicious greeting in the woods. Finally one old lumberman became exasperated by the whole affair. When asked to give his nationality he replied 'The Republic of Madawaksa'. Other lumbermen took up the joke and elected the Mayor of Edmunston to be their President.

To this day the lumbering heritage of Madawaska, and most of inland New Brunswick, is celebrated in the lively Foire Brayonne festival. Some outsiders might say that the good natured fun of the logging celebrations are rather rowdy, but the Madawaskans enjoy themselves and perpetuate their cultural origins. There are log cutting competitions and log rolling takes place on the river. Folksongs are sung in competition and traditional skills are exhibited.

Further down the Saint John River are lands inhabited by people of a very different culture, though once again the growing power of the United States had a hand in its creation. When the 13 American colonies rebelled against British rule many of their inhabitants disagreed with this action. They preferred to remain loyal to the king and legitimate government. When the rebels finally won the struggle, many of the Loyalists fled rather than face the hostility of the new country.

The vast majority of them came to New Brunswick, for it was the nearest British colony to remain attached to the mother country. In all some 50,000 Loyalists came to New Brunswick to carve new homes for themselves. They rapidly built rough wooden farm houses and cleared the forests for agriculture. In the early days the Loyalist settlements must have presented a strange sight to visitors. The houses and farms were as primitive as most frontier settlements, but the Loyalists had brought the luxuries of their old homes with them. It was not unusual to find a log cabin illuminated by silver candlesticks and the family dining off fine china.

The Loyalist days are recreated at Kings Landing Historical Settlement which stands on the banks of the Saint John. The reconstructed buildings and the costumes of the staff concentrate on the period after 1820 when the Loyalists were well established in their new home.

Loyalist origins are also celebrated during the July festival of Loyalist Days in the city of Saint John. The city came into being when 3,000 Loyalists landed on the coast on 11th May 1783 and set up a tent town which gradually grew into the modern city of 87,000 souls. The area where the first settlers landed is now known as Market Square and is still the heart of the city. The old 19th century buildings of the square have been recently restored and form a delightful shopping and dining area. The towering office developments of the city climb into the sky nearby, casting their shadows over the old square.

Prince Edward Island

In contrast to the turbulent origins of other Maritime Provinces Prince Edward Island had very peaceful beginnings. Indeed, its early history was so untroubled that very little of it was recorded at all.

The great French explorer Jacques Cartier discovered the island in 1534 and named it Ile St Jean. For the next two centuries no European settlement was attempted, but in 1720 a band of 300 Frenchmen arrived and established a farming community near the site of modern Charlottetown. Thirty years later a number of Acadians from Nova Scotia settled on the island. But the British were as concerned about Frenchmen on Ile St Jean as much as about Frenchmen in Nova Scotia. In 1758 a British force arrived and established a military presence. Many of the Acadians left.

The few who remained lived around the shores of Malpeque Bay. This broad, shallow bay is almost cut off from the open sea by extensive sandbanks and mudflats. The waters are, therefore, remarkably sheltered and in summer the sun heats the shallows until they reach almost bath temperature. It is in the waters of this bay that early fishermen first came across the famous Malpeque oyster. These medium sized, cupped oysters spend their lives attached to the rocks and pebbles of the seabed by a tough fibrous strand. Vast numbers of them are destined to end their lives on the dinner plates of residents and visitors to Prince Edward Island.

The oysters have become famous throughout the world for their exquisite flavour and the consistent quality of the catches. Indeed one cookery book of 1907 while recommending ordinary oysters as a food for invalids as they can be easily digested warns that Malpeques should be reserved for the healthy who can appreciate them. Originally the oysters were found only in the bay. More recently oyster beds have been established in coves and bays around the island so that the supply of Malpeques has increased enormously. Many thousands are flown out each year to grace the tables of Montreal, Quebec and Toronto.

It is not only oysters which are brought up from the sea on Prince Edward Island. Lobsters are plentiful and form the basis for the traditional 'feeds'. These special meals concentrate heavily on local produce. The first course is invariably clam chowder which is followed by boiled lobster and huge bowls of mashed potatoes. In addition to these staples the Feed may include a variety of pickles, salads and soft fruits. Bread is another standby on such occasions, preferably freshly baked from local wheatflour. Several restaurants in and around Malpeque recreate these family celebrations for visitors.

Food is not the only attraction of Malpeque. There are also rolling miles of beaches which attract hordes of bathers in the summer. The spreading Malpeque Gardens are another favourite with visitors, featuring rose gardens, hundreds of varieties of dahlias and a restored windmill. Beyond the confines of the bay the sandy beaches and coves run onwards before turning northward to form North Cape.

The Cape is constantly battered by the tidal drifts of Northumberland Strait and the Gulf of St Lawrence and the long Atlantic rollers. The soft sandstone cannot withstand the pounding and is constantly eroding, falling into the sea to be ground up into sand and swept eastwards to be deposited in spits and bars along the coast.

The long beaches of the southern coast are the home of one of the more unusual products of Prince Edward Island; a seaweed which is called moss. The seaweed is washed up from the sea by storms and gales. After such blowy weather the locals turn out to collect the weed and carry it inland where it is laid out in fields and along roadsides. Once dried the weed is bagged up and sold as Irish moss, a useful addition to sandy garden soils.

But the most famous product of Prince Edward Island is probably neither the Malpeque oyster nor the Irish moss. It is the potato. Vast quantities of potatoes are produced each year, far more than the islanders can actually eat. Most are exported to the rest of Canada, being particularly prized as seed stock. So extensive are the potato lands that Prince Edward Island has been referred to as 'two beaches separated by a potato field'.

But there is far more to the Island, as locals know the province, even from the point of view of crops. Of the 450,000 acres of farmland just under half is given over to potatoes. Other areas of Prince Edward Island's fertile red soil is covered by sweeping grain fields which have made the Island self-sufficient in wheat and barley. The remainder of the farmland is given over to blueberries, raspberries and vegetables. The great fertility of the rich, red soil is amply reflected in the dinner tables of the province which carry more home-produced variety than those of most other provinces.

In fact so much of this low-lying island is agricultural that it has the highest population density of all the Canadian provinces. There are no extensive, uninhabited wilderness areas on Prince Edward Island, only rolling hills and shady hollows.

The quiet rural atmosphere of the island has been celebrated in one of the greatest of books ever written for children. *Anne of Green Gables* was written by a local woman, Lucy Maud Montgomery and published in 1908. It has remained a firm favourite ever since and has been made into films and television serials.

The story concerns a young orphan girl who is brought up by relatives on a quiet Prince Edward Island farm. The actual farmhouse, in reality owned by cousins of Lucy Maud Montgomery, can still be seen and visited. The small white house is suitably adorned with green gables and contains various memorabilia concerning the authoress and her works. Montgomery's birthplace stands a few miles away in New London as another shrine to the writer.

More spectacular is the annual musical version of the novel performed at the Charlottetown Festival which runs from July to October. The festival, as a whole, being one of the most famous and prestigious festivals of the performing arts in Canada.

Charlottetown is the capital of the province, but its main claim to fame is that it was the birthplace of a united Canada. Until 1864 the various provinces were entirely separate colonies linked only by their allegiance to Britain. In that year, however, representatives of the various colonies met in Province House in Charlottetown to discuss terms of a union or confederation. After lengthy discussion a workable scheme was produced and, in 1867, was put into operation by an Act of Parliament in Britain. Ironically Prince Edward Island refused to join until 1873.

Province House still stands, and still serves as the meeting place for the provincial legislature. The finely crafted sandstone structure has a Classical facade and is laid out expressly for the business of law making. The chamber where the 'Fathers of Confederation' met in 1864 has been restored to period style and is open to the public.

Next to the Province House is a startlingly modern arts centre, paid for by the whole nation in 1964. In addition to the more usual theatres and art gallery, the centre houses a library a museum and a restaurant. The building contrasts architecturally not only with the Province House, but also with much of central Charlottetown.

There is little heavy industry in the city. Most of the 30,000 citizens earn a living in government or from tourism, while a few are employed in food processing. There is, therefore, little pressure to redevelop the older parts of the city, indeed they are seen as a tourist asset.

The main business of Charlottetown is its port, through which the majority of the Island's produce leaves for the mainland. The older sections of the waterfront, with their Victorian warehouses and shops, have been restored as a charming shopping and leisure area. The nearby Rockford Square is sheltered by 110 trees, planted over a century ago. Many of these streets are lit by gaslight, which casts a warm, soft glow at night. As a final reminder of the past there is still employed a town crier who wanders the streets making various announcements.

Acutely aware of how important tourism is to the island, the provincial government has laid out three day long drives. Together the routes take motorists around most of the island and link the majority of the attractions.

The most westerly is Lady Slipper Drive which begins at an information centre near Summerside. The route runs north to skirt Malpeque Bay towards Port Hill where a shipbuilding museum includes a partially built schooner displaying the construction techniques and skills of the old-time shipwrights who produced fishing ships in the bay. The Lady Slipper Drive than heads northwards to round North Cape on a road which has been moved several times to avoid the encroaching sea. It then runs along the west coast to West Point and so back to Summerside.

The Blue Heron Drive runs in a long loop around the central region of the island, between the two inlets of Malpeque and West River. It can be picked up at almost any point, but most prefer to begin at Charlottetown. The first place of note is the Prince Edward Island National Park, which runs for 25 miles along the northern coast between Grand Tracadie and Cavendish. The park contains a complex and strangely haunting coastline. There are numerous headlands, bays and high bluffs but the shoreline has been softened by the vast amounts of sand brought by the tidal run from North Cape. Broad beaches, high sand dunes and extensive salt marshes spread below the bluffs and between the headlands, making the national park a region of great variety, and the home to many species of seabird.

The Blue Heron Drive leaves the park and cuts south across the island to Borden. The coast of Northumberland Strait, separating the Island from the mainland, is studded with bathing beaches. Though rather less scenic than those of the north coast, the Northumberland beaches are by far the most popular on the island. They are broad and sandy while the sea which washes them forms a backwash of the powerful offshore Gulf Stream. They are, therefore, much warmer than other waters. It was on this coast that the first European settlers landed, and their impact can still be seen in the ruined rampart of an 18th century British fortress.

The third drive has been labelled Kings Byway and, like the Blue Heron, loops around from Charlottetown. Much of the landscape through which it runs is less intensively farmed than the rest of the island and large areas are given over to grazing. The many inlets and coves of the east coast are occupied by fishing villages very like those to be found on the mainland Maritimes.

Some of the villages originated with settlements of Scottish highlanders and continue to preserve the culture, most noticeably with annual highland games and more frequent ceilidhs, or village dances. Other places are more commercial. North Lake prides itself being the world centre for the sport of tuna fishing on line. Many charter boats are specially equipped with heavy rods and lines and hire themselves out for the day. Some of the larger bluefin tuna weigh over 1200 pounds, making them among the largest of the game fish.

In some ways Prince Edward Island is untypical of the Maritimes. Its fishing communities are a minority and have little cultural influence. Its rich agricultural land covers most of the island and there is virtually nothing in the way of wilderness regions for the outdoor sportsman. But in one essential way it is a typical Maritime Province. It has a character entirely its own. It is a contradictory feature which unites the Maritimes. They are similar only because they are so different from each other and from the rest of the world.

Nova Scotia has long been famous for its fishing craft. Built from local timber, the boats huddle in numerous bays and inlets around the rugged coast of the province. The most picturesque of these small fishing harbours are to be found along the rocky southern coast of the peninsula and include such well-known spots as Shelburne (above), Indian Harbour (previous pages) and Peggy's Cove (overleaf). On the rugged Cape Breton Island stands the town of Glace Bay (top), which has a small fishing fleet, but is better known for its coal mines which reach far out under the ocean. Facing page: Port Mouton.

Facing page: Blue Rocks. Above: The Cabot Trail which runs for 180 miles around the coast of Cape Breton Island, taking in some of Nova Scotia's finest scenery. The route is circular and can be picked up at any point, though most people prefer to start at Sydney, and is best appreciated over two or even three days. The sheer cliffs along which the road passes make for both magnificent scenery and hair-raising driving. The route was named after John Cabot, the Italian mariner working for England who, it is claimed, was the first European to sight these shores. Top: the small craft and boat houses of Blue Rocks. Overleaf: Indian Harbour, which was once an important site for the Micmac Indians who inhabited Nova Scotia when John Cabot called here more than four centuries ago. The Micmacs now live on reservations on Cape Breton and near Truro.

The height of the tides which are experienced around the coasts of Nova Scotia is shown by the size of the wharves at Freeport (this page). Facing page top: lobster pots lie stacked on a jetty at Louisbourg. Facing page bottom: The sun sets across St Margaret's Bay at Indian Harbour. Overleaf: The brightly painted houses and broad bay of Lunenburg, a town of some 3,000 inhabitants. Lunenburg lies near the centre of the province's Atlantic Coast and has long been a focus for the fishing industry. Today the town holds the internationally famous Fishing Museum of the Atlantic which concentrates on the history of fishing on the Grand Banks. The museum is unusually housed, being contained in three ships the *Cape North*, the *Reo II* and the *Theresa E. Connor*, the last schooner to fish the Grand Banks.

Louisbourg, at the southeastern tip of Cape Breton Island, was the site of France's most powerful 18th century naval fortress in the New World. The site was chosen to contain a harbour and fortified supply depot which would form a key part in the defences of French Canada. The ships which were based at Louisbourg were able to range widely across the mouth of the St Lawrence and along the eastern seaboard, denying the trade routes to ships of other nations and snapping up prizes during time of war. The fortress finally fell to the British General Wolfe in 1758 and, after the fall of Quebec, was demolished in 1760. Much of the fortress has now been restored to its original condition and visitors can wander around in the company of costumed staff and inspect 18th century military hardware. Overleaf: Peggy's Cove.

The powerful tides and indented coast of Nova Scotia make the inshore waters particularly dangerous for the unwary. Tidal streams are deflected by bays and torn apart by headlands to form races of frightening speed which can change direction swiftly. Locals know the tides well and can take advantage of them to move their craft along, but strangers are likely to be swept into danger. The coast has therefore been studded with lighthouses such as those at Peggy's Cove (right) and Neil's Harbour (overleaf) to aid navigation. These pages: Peggy's Cove, the charming Nova Scotian fishing village which is visited by thousands every year yet which has resolutely refused to be spoilt by the influx. The community's only concession to tourism is a solitary restaurant for hungry travellers.

The rugged Cape Breton Island (these pages) is a land of rocky hills, tumbling mountain streams and dense forests. Some of the most inaccessible lands, on the high plateau near Ingonish, has been set aside as a National Park and includes such sights as the Mary Ann Falls (above left). But the park does not have a monopoly on scenery, nor on waterfalls as Beuloch Bann Falls (above right) and

Lake O'Law (facing page) illustrate. The rugged scenery fits in well with the distinctly Scottish feel of the island. During the 19th century many Scottish crofters, forced to leave their homes by their landlords, came to Nova Scotia in the hope of finding a new home. Most did, and their descendants live here to this day.

Fishing has been a major industry in Nova Scotia right from the earliest days of European settlement. The most valuable catch, pound for pound, is lobster and lobster pots can be found stacked at small villages throughout the province, such as Le Hare Island (facing page) and Mushaboom Bay (top). One of the largest centres for the lobster industry is Shelburne, near the extreme southern tip of the province. Here live lobsters are graded, weighed and packed for their journey to high class restaurants throughout the country. Because sorting must be done when the animals are alive, they first have their sharp claws firmly clamped shut with elastic bands (left). Herring fishing, (above) at Lockeport, lacks the glamour of lobster catching, but can be equally profitable. Overleaf: Farmland near Avonport.

Despite the abundance of stone in Nova Scotia, the province's commonest building material is wood. Indeed at traditional settlements, such as Kingsburg (top), Rissers Beach (above), Hacketts Cove (facing page top) and West Dover (facing page bottom), virtually no other material is in sight. Homes, boathouses and outbuildings are all timber-framed and walled with shingles or weatherboarding. Even the jetties are built of stout logs, lashed together into boxes and filled with stones for stability. The reason for the dominance of timber is the fact that most of the province is covered by conifer forest, which provides wood which is cheap, easy to work and close to the site of use. There is really no reason why the Nova Scotians should look any further.

Nova Scotia is best known for its Scottish heritage derived from settlers of the last century, indeed the province's name is Latin for 'New Scotland'. But the province has a much more varied population than such a history would indicate, a fact shown by the names of various towns and villages. The village of Grand Pré (right) has a French name meaning 'large meadow' and dates back to the time when the French owned Nova Scotia. The growing of vines and the production of wine in the area emphasises the French culture. Tiverton (above and facing page top) was named after a famous town in Devon county, England, while Crescent Beach (top) has a descriptive name given it by English settlers. Lunenburg (facing page bottom) has a name derived from German settlers. Overleaf: Lower Blomidon.

Halifax (these pages and overleaf) is the largest city in Nova Scotia with a population of around 120,000. This bustling port and industrial city dates back to 1749 when the British founded the city as a balance to the French settlement at Louisbourg on Cape Breton. The Old Town Clock (facing page bottom) is one of the most distinctive landmarks of Halifax. It stands between the fortified

Citadel and the town. Another link with the past is the schooner *Bluenose II* (above left) which is usually berthed in the harbour, but often sets sail on goodwill visits abroad. The Angus L. Macdonald Bridge (top) was opened in 1955 to ease travel across the harbour, but so great is the pressure that a second bridge has been added and ferries are still active.

The characteristic bare, windswept appearance of Nova Scotian fishing villages is largely a product of the soil. Around most bays the soils are thin and poor, with bare rock pushing through in many areas. Only scrubby grassland and stunted forests can survive in such places, as at Romkey Pond (facing page bottom), Main a Dieu (above), Bush Island (top) and Prospect Village (overleaf), all of which support small, but thriving fishing fleets. Inland the scenery changes dramatically. The hills are blanketed with thick forests while the river valleys have a deep, rich soil which can be ploughed and sown with arable crops, as at Norths (facing page top).

The rugged landscape and numerous streams of inland Nova Scotia made it an ideal area for the construction of watermills, such as that shown (top) at Balmoral Mills in Chichester County. These mills did not only grind flour, but were also harnessed to saw timber. The same landscape has made life difficult for modern golfers. At Chester (facing page top) and Guysborough (facing page bottom) fairways have been laid out on relatively flat coastal lands, cleared of forest. Chester is a particularly famous sports resort having, in addition to golf, facilities for sport fishing, yachting and other pastimes. The lands around the Minas Basin (above), near Medord, have been cleared for arable land and pasture.

Though its coasts are dotted with fishing villages, Prince Edward Island is not as dependent on the sea as other Maritime Provinces. Its rich fertile land supports a prosperous agriculture growing a wide variety of crops. Not only is Prince Edward Island less mountainous and endowed with more fertile soil, it also has a much better climate than the other Maritimes. There are more frostfree days, well over 130, and more reliable rainfall than elsewhere, both of which make the island a more secure agricultural area. Facing page: Wood Islands Lighthouse. Top: Lupins growing wild near Kingsboro. Above: A field of barley. Overleaf: North Rustico Harbour, a noted resort with a fine beach and watersports facilities.

Prince Edward Island, with its low hills and fertile soil, is built on a bed of ancient red sandstones which date back some 400 million years. Across most of the island the sandstone is overlain by soil and crops, but around the coast the rock can be clearly seen. Facing page bottom: a helicopter hovers over the cliffs of Cavendish, a noted seaside resort. Overleaf: The waves batter the crumbling sandstone near Park Corner, where Lucy Maud Montgomery, author of *Anne of Green Gables*, lived and where her house is now a museum operated by her descendants. Top: Farmland near the north coast of the island. Above: Fishermen put to sea from Northlake Harbour to set their lobster traps. Facing page top: The sun sinks behind a typically broad bay on Prince Edward Island's north coast.

Prince Edward Island has been described, rather sweepingly, as a huge potato field surrounded by beaches. Though the description is far from true, it is fact that the island is dominated by potato fields, like those near Kensington (facing page bottom). Indeed there is about 1 acre of land under potatoes for each inhabitant of the island and around 50% of farmers rely on the crop for their livelihood. The climate on the island is almost ideal for the potato, being warm enough to allow a heavy yield, but cool enough to keep pests at bay. There is, however, more to the Island's economy than one crop, and dairy farming (facing page top) is increasing in importance. During the summer the cattle are grazed outside while enough hay and silage can be produced for winter feed. Above: Peggy's Cove, Nova Scotia.

Although Prince Edward Island relies heavily on agriculture for its wealth, tourism is growing in importance. Thousands of visitors flock across the Northumberland Strait each summer to enjoy themselves on the Island. The Islanders are awake to the needs of the visitors and have laid out three scenic drives, as well as developing some beach resorts, such as Cavendish (overleaf). A long stretch of the northern coastline has been set aside as the Prince Edward Island National Park (left), to ensure the preservation of its red cliffs and long, sandy beaches. Much of the interior remains undeveloped, offering unspoilt scenery to the visitor. Above: The James Yeo Homestead. Top: Lupins near Lakeville. Facing page bottom: grainfields in Kings County.

More than half a million tourists visit Prince Edward Island each year, and many of them make for Rustico (this page) in the centre of the north coast. The village makes an ideal base, being less than an hour from Charlottetown and even closer to Prince Edward Island National Park. Most of the farmhouses, and many private homes have guest rooms, while there are also campsites, motels and inns. However, other holidaymakers search for the quiet isolation for which the Maritimes have become famous, and find it on Panmure Island (facing page), just off the east coast near Georgetown. A few guesthouses and campsites cater to visitors, but these do little to detract from the peaceful, atmosphere of the place.

These pages: Charlottetown, the capital of Prince Edward Island, which was named after Queen Charlotte, consort of King George III. The city contains many fine monuments and buildings, including the war memorial (top), Government House (above left), Queen Square (above right) and Beaconsfield Mansion (facing page top). But the most historically significant structure is Confederation House (facing page bottom) where the details of the Canadian federation were first discussed. The meeting convened in 1864, when the American civil war threatened to drag Canada into a maelstrom of violence and annexation. In Charlottetown, and later at Quebec, the Canadian colonies called for virtual independence within the British Empire, which was gained in 1867. Overleaf: Cavendish Beach.

Prince Edward Island. Top: Lobster pots dry in the sun on a dock in Naufrage Harbour. Large numbers of lobsters are caught off the coast each year, providing the central dish for the famous Prince Edward Island lobster suppers. These festive occasions are generally family affairs, but some local restaurants are now organising them for the paying tourist. Above: West Point Lighthouse, in Cedar Dunes Provincial Park, which marks the northeastern corner of Prince Edward Island and the entrance to Northumberland Strait. Left: Point Prim Lighthouse. Facing page top: Farmland near Kinlock. Facing page bottom: A long, shallow inlet near the small resort of New London.

The phenomenon of longshore drift is common off Prince Edward Island and is seen nowhere better than at New London (facing page top). The tides and currents which run along the north coast of the island carry with them large amounts of sand eroded out of the red sandstone cliffs. Where the currents enter a bay they slow down, dropping their load at the mouth of the inlet. Gradually the deposits grow up until a long sandbar is formed, pointing in the direction of the current. The spit at New London has become so stable that grasses now grow on its landward side. Top: A dairy farm overlooking Orby Head and West River. Above: A church near Cavendish. Facing page bottom: A beautifully preserved church near Kensington.

These pages: Prince Edward Island. Facing page top: Hay drying in a field near Lower Newton. Hay is an important winter food for the dairy herds of the Island and is produced in large quantities. Facing page bottom: A causeway cuts across an inlet near Springbrook. Such long, low bridges are common on the Island where roads would otherwise need to make long detours inland. Top: Lobsterpots stacked near the lighthouse on the ominously named Shipwreck Point. The regular flash of the lighthouse helps to keep craft clear of this dangerous headland. Above: The crumbling coastline at Cape Tryon. The continual battering of the waves is eroding the shoreline and eventually the houses will fall into the sea.

Previous pages: Lush pastureland and hay fields near the New Brunswick town of Grand Falls, one of several officially bilingual communities in the province. With a population of 85,000 Saint John (these pages) is not only the capital of New Brunswick, but also its largest city. In recent years a large-scale restoration of the older parts of the city have returned them to popular use, attracting visitors from far beyond the immediate area. Market Square (top and facing page) marks the spot where the first settlers landed and has a pleasing mix of old and new styles. The nearby waterfront (above) contains modern buildings in traditional style. Overleaf: A tiny hamlet near Smith Creek.

New Brunswick's Seal Cove (facing page top) was, no doubt, named for the sea mammals which once gathered here. Today's fishermen would probably not welcome a return of the seals which have been known to tear nets to get at the fish inside. Facing page bottom: A lobster pound on Campobello Island, which is actually easier to reach via the bridge from Maine, than by the ferry from New Brunswick. Top: The sun dips towards the horizon over Indian Island in the Kennebecasis River. Above: A covered bridge over Milksit Inlet on the Kingston Peninsula. Covered bridges were once very common in New Brunswick, their roofs keeping the bridge free of snow and ice during winter, but now many are falling into disrepair and are being replaced.

New Brunswickers are particularly conscious of their national origins and do much to preserve the identity of their forbears. At the Village Acadien Historique near Bathurst (top left) the lifestyle of the area's original Acadian settlers is recreated. The Acadians, French settlers of the 17th and 18th century, were expelled by the British in 1755 when war between Britain and France flared up and the Acadians were suspected of aiding the French. The Village Historique concentrates on the period between 1780 and 1890, when small groups of Acadians returned to New Brunswick to live under British rule. At Kings Landing, on the Saint John River, the lifestyle of 19th century British settlers is likewise recreated (above left, above right, top right and facing page).

In the aftermath of the American War of Independence many Loyalists left the newly created United States to find sanctuary in New Brunswick. The lives of these people, struggling to make a home in a hostile environment, is recreated at Kings Landing Historical Settlement (these pages), near Fredericton. Some of the buildings are new, but built with traditional materials to original styles, but others are genuine period pieces moved here when they became threatened with destruction by the rising waters of the Mactaquac Dam. The Settlement is staffed by costumed actors who are trained to speak and behave as if they have stepped out of the past. Kings Landing is a major tourist attraction which is open throughout the summer. Overleaf: Farmland near Glassville.

The small New Brunswick town of Hartland is charming, but unremarkable except for its covered bridge. Spanning the broad Saint John River, the bridge measures 1,282 feet from end to end and is supported on six piers. The bridge, which features an unusual separate covered walkway, was built in 1897 and has been restored at intervals. The people of Seal Cove (above), on Grand Manan Island rely heavily on fishing for their livelihoods, sending out small fishing boats, such as that (right) in the Bay of Fundy, and spreading weirnets around the coast. Seagulls flock behind the craft as the fishermen gut their catch and fling the innards overboard. Grand Manan Island is the largest island in the Bay of Fundy and is a superb bird sanctuary where ornithologists have counted over 250 species.

Nearly 90% of New Brunswick is covered by forestlands where the soil is too poor or sloping for agricultural use. However, some of the river valleys have rich, fertile soils which can easily support large farms, as is shown by the landscape around Drummond (facing page bottom). Elsewhere people make a living from the sea, catching fish or laying lobster pots (facing page top). Top: dark storm clouds gather over East Quoddy Head Lighthouse, emphasising the need for such navigational aids on this tough, rugged coast. Above: The faint lights of human settlement glimmer across the bay from Gowdola Point. Overleaf: The Saint John River at Fredericton.

The Village Acadien Historique (top and above), just west of
Caraquet, contains 30 houses which are built and furnished in the
style of the Acadian farmers of the 19th century. Costumed staff
work with farm implements of the period and live out the daily
routines of the original Acadians. Left: A woman combing wool at
Kings Landing Historical Settlement. The broad, hooked combs
untangle the woollen fibres and pull them into line, ready for
spinning into thread. Dorchester, at the neck of the isthmus leading
to Nova Scotia, contains the historic Keillor House (facing page)
which is furnished after the fashion of the last century and is carefully
maintained.

The Kingston Peninsula, on New Brunswick's southern coast is a charming area containing many fine old houses, such as that (facing page top) and churches, like St James's Church at Long Reach (above). Facing page bottom: The covered bridge at Hartland in the Saint John Valley, which is the longest in the world. The solid concrete piers are canted on the upstream side to break the force of the spring meltwater floods. Top: Fertile farmland near Drummond. Overleaf: The Head Harbour Lighthouse on Campobello Island in the Bay of Fundy. In 1767 the island was given by the British government to the naval captain William Owens in recompense for the loss of his arm in action. Captain Owens's house still stands and is open to the public.

St Andrew's (facing page top and right) prides itself as being one of the most English towns in New Brunswick. It is a small town, with only 2,000 inhabitants and 600 buildings, many of which date back over 150 years, but with a surplus of character. The Carleton Matello Tower (facing page bottom) was built to protect Saint John Harbour when the war of 1812 flared with the United States. Following a pattern for coastal defence forts already common in Britain, the tower is a circular gun platform the lower storeys of which were used as barracks and ammunition stores. Above: The Officers' Quarters in Fredericton which were built in 1825 and now house a museum. Top: Roosevelt Cottage, holiday home of the United States' President Franklin D. Roosevelt, which is now a museum dedicated to the memory of its former owner.

Above: Deep Cove on Grand Manan Island, New Brunswick. It is in sheltered bays and inlets such as this that the dulse seaweed grows. At low tide islanders gather to collect the purple seaweed and take it inland for drying and packing. The seaweed is a popular snack, not only on Grand Manan, but throughout New Brunswick. It has a strong, salty flavour which is irresistible to some, but only too resistible to others. Top: The forests around Apohaqui. Facing page top: An evening flight of birds dot the sky above Robichaud. Facing page bottom: The curious Flowerpot Rocks of the aptly named The Rocks Provincial Park on Hopewell Cape. At low tide the highly eroded bases are revealed, but at high tide they are covered and the rocks appear to be rather unremarkable islets. Overleaf: Forest homes near Waterford.

Facing page top: Forest and farmland near Moncton, New Brunswick. The town of Moncton was named after Colonel Robert Monckton who captured the area from the French in 1755, although the official documents misspelled his name. It is now, ironically, the heart of the Acadian culture over which Monckton won his victories. Facing page bottom: The sun sets over the sea near Petit Rocher.

Top: Swallowtail Lighthouse stands guard on its rocky headland on Grand Manan Island. Above: A small covered bridge crosses a deep stream amid lush pasture near Sussex Corner. Overleaf: The late afternoon sun spreads long shadows across the landscape near Florenceville.

At Waterford (top) the flatter areas have been cleared for farmland while more precipitous slopes have been left with their native forest cover. Above: The fields around Drummond, one of the most fertile areas of New Brunswick. Facing page top: A long straight road cuts its way across the landscape near Glassville. Facing page bottom: A rail fence snakes its way into a valley near Smith Creek. These fences are quick and easy to build and gain much of their formidable strength from the bracing of the angles. Where these fences mark boundaries between neighbouring farms disputes have sometimes arisen as to who owns the land between the kinks.

Above: Swimmers and sunbathers crowd Parlee Beach near Shediac, New Brunswick. The inshore waters here are very shallow and cut off from the open sea by extensive sandbars. The sun is therefore able to heat the water up to the warmest it reaches off the Maritimes. These same waters contain rich lobster grounds where enormous quantities of these creatures are caught. Shediac holds a lobster festival each July when vast quantities of the delicacy are consumed and the town celebrates its self-styled title of 'Lobster Capital of the World'. Facing page top: Musquash Harbour Lighthouse, near Saint John, on the Bay of Fundy. Facing page bottom: Farms near Holmesville. Overleaf: Drummond.

New Brunswick has two great rivers; the Saint John and the Miramichi. The Saint John, (top) at Hartland, rises in the United States, forms part of the border with Maine and flows into the sea at Saint John. It is a river which flows across the most intensively farmed lands in the province and passes through three major cities. The Mirimachi, (above and facing page) at Doaktown, is very different. It flows through wilder, more rugged countryside and towns with populations no larger than 10,000. The Miramichi is famous as a sporting river and attracts thousands of sportsmen each year. It is particularly well known for its salmon (facing page) which move upstream in large numbers each year and, unlike their Pacific cousins, return several years in succession.

Newfoundland is the most distinctive of the Maritime Provinces, having only joined Canada in 1949 and being closer to Europe than it is to Vancouver. The harsh landscape and climate of the island have forced its inhabitants to develop a unique lifestyle, based upon the sea and its produce. Previous pages: Fishermen inspect their nets at Pools Cove. Top: The forest-hugged outport of Mooring Cove. Above: The inlet at Hillgrade. Facing page top: Waves pound the shore at Pouch Cove. Facing page bottom: Houses hug the shore at Jenkins Cove. Overleaf: The pure blue waters of Greenspond on Greenspond Island.

Trinity (top, above and facing page bottom) is one of the oldest settlements on Newfoundland. It was discovered on Trinity Sunday, hence its name, in the year 1500 and by 1615 was sufficiently important to host a Court of the Admiralty. The actual date of the first settlement here, however, remains obscure. Today it has a population of less than 500 and some reconstructed forts and guns.

The waters of Trinity Bay are famous for their whales, and many visitors come here solely with the hope of sighting one of these impressive creatures. Facing page top: Harbour Breton, whose name commemorates its French connection. Overleaf: The boathouses, jetties and fishing craft of New Bonaventure.

The magnificent natural harbour on which St John's (these pages) stands was discovered by John Cabot on St John's Day 1497, and so gained its name. The large, deepwater harbour is entered by a narrow gap in the cliffs which was once strongly fortified and covered by heavy cannon. Although St John's is one of the oldest cities in the Americas there are very few old buildings here, due to a series of devastating fires which practically levelled the town last century.

Perhaps the most imposing structure in the town is the Basilica of St John the Baptist, whose twin towers dominate most views of the area. Top: The fine war memorial which commemorates the men of the town who gave their lives in two World Wars. Above: The startlingly clean lines of the Confederation Building. Overleaf: Curzon Village on Bonne Bay.

The most easterly point of Canada, indeed of the whole American continent, is Cape Spear (this page), which has now been declared a National Historic Park. The chill waters off the headland are famous for their whales, which gather here to feed on the huge quantities of tiny crustaceans, named krill, which swarm in the sea. Facing page top: The setting sun silhouettes the lighthouse on Long Point. Facing page bottom: The brightly painted lighthouse on Crow Head. Newfoundlanders often paint houses and other coastal structures with distinctive colours so that they can be used as navigation aids by seamen, who are very often members of their own families. Overleaf: The small fishing community of Pools Cove.

Many of the early explorers of Newfoundland were Catholics who expressed their piety by giving their discoveries religious names. It was in this way that Conception Bay (top) and Notre Dame Bay (above) became so called. The English who named Pouch Cove (facing page bottom) were rather more secularly minded. Bonavista Bay (facing page top) has a name which means 'beautiful view'. According to tradition it was given this name by John Cabot as this was his first sight of land after crossing the Atlantic. Overleaf: The community of Belleoram, continuously inhabited since 1759.

Since the Second World War, after which Newfoundland joined Canada, large amounts of money have been spent on improving local roads. Especially important was the construction of the TransCanada Highway from Channel Port-aux-Basques to St John's, and many smaller outports have now become accessible by road for the first time ever. However, it still remains true that many settlements are best reached by sea and the level of boat-ownership is more impressive than the percentage of Newfoundlanders who own cars. Above: Norris Point on Bonne Bay. Top and facing page bottom: Newtown. Facing page top: Gillsport.

Top left, above and facing page: Atlantic puffins in breeding plumage. Left: A pair of tufted puffins perched on a crag. Top right: A pair of horned puffins, which take their name from the curious crests above their eyes. The puffin, of which there are several species in Canadian coastlands, is a member of the auk family, which is spread throughout the northern hemisphere. They are powerful fliers and the puffin is often seen returning to its nest with several fish grasped in its bill. Outside the breeding season, the plumage of the puffins becomes duller and the bill loses its spectacular striped appearance. The change is no doubt an aid to camouflage, and young birds have the duller plumage year round.

The heavy rainfall and mountainous interior of Newfoundland make ideal conditions for waterfalls of breathtaking power and beauty. The Gull Island Falls (facing page) are located on Conception Bay, just a few miles west of St John's. The much more powerful Churchill Falls (top) cascade down a cliff in the rugged interior of Labrador. The falls have been harnessed to a hydro-electric power station which provides energy for developing local industries. Covering much of the St Lawrence coast of western Newfoundland is Gros Morne National Park, which includes some truly spectacular scenery, such as Ten Mile Pond (overleaf) and the Rocky Coast (above).

Photographers' Index